Tiny Extravaganzas

ARROWSMITH
PRESS

Tiny Extravaganzas

poems by Diane Mehta

Tiny Extravaganzas
Diane Mehta

ISBN: 979-8-9879241-1-2

Boston — New York — San Francisco — Baghdad
San Juan — Kyiv — Istanbul — Santiago, Chile
Beijing — Paris — London — Cairo — Madrid
Milan — Melbourne — Jerusalem — Darfur

11 Chestnut St.
Medford, MA 02155

arrowsmithpress@gmail.com
www.arrowsmithpress.com

The fifty-third Arrowsmith book
was typeset & designed by Ezra Fox
for Askold Melnyczuk & Alex Johnson
in EB Garamond and Optima fonts

Cover art: The Metropolitan Museum of Art, New York
Comb, French or Italian, 15th or 16th century
Gift of J. Pierpont Morgan, 1917

for Ivan and Jerry

ONE

TWO

THREE

When B. sat down at the piano and made
A transparence in which we heard music, made music
In which we heard transparent sounds, did he play
All sorts of notes? Or did he play only one
In an ecstasy of its associates,
Variations in the tones of a single sound,
The last, or sounds so single they seemed one?

-Wallace Stevens

World is crazier and more of it than we think,
Incorrigibly plural. I peel and portion
A tangerine and spit the pips and feel
The drunkenness of things being various.

-Louis MacNeice

ONE

RENDEZVOUS

You have to lose all beginnings to know where the story
really begins, all the wandering by accident or design
a way to find your tongue. Pull the everything around you.
Once upon a time, first love fed gristle in your mouth—
you Dewey Decimal it as experience, world your catalog.
Suffering is never wrong, and loving is entanglements of grand.

Remember red-sledding down back yard winter hills
when temperatures fell in daggers on the windowsills
and free was air in knotted hair? Cold snap at warp speed
on our cheeks. Wasn't it the greatest show on earth
to sit there with our mothers, warming our hands on cider
that burned our lips, frostflower etchings on the windows?

After all the acrobatics and plot twists promising new
promiselands, how do you feel about the story now?
Hasn't it changed, aging in its cage, and haven't you?
What truth resists! It hides in the angles of its triangles
then punches its way to the center, guffawing at its crimes—
the soul is still the same while it makes a king of you.

GALA NOISE

I

All morning the off-tune brimful singing
rruh-khee, scre-chee, cruk-ah, uh-hoo, zurrah
clangs a ruckus over the dream of a collective tempo
and for a fraction of a second, we hear the affections
of a world aligned.

You'd think the sounds were from another century,
knowledge so clearly carried through them.

They resemble the embodied voices of mycelium
sending instructions about, Morse code for roots
distributing seminal beliefs
as if they were explaining the strictures of priesthood
or the water table for static-screech cicadas
waiting for their stage appearance every twelve years.

If only we, like all creatures,
were untroubled by catastrophe,
and allowed the soil
to extract, from our marrow-bone bodies,
words that disappoint and words that rhyme.

II

Every day at noon, the crystal mist burns off
high up by the campanile.
Lackadaisical days, sensational ways to feel
in greens and deeper greens.

But the warbling hoot and hiss and serenades we hear
convulse with something sinister we share,
that inner wrangling
shrieking on the sunglow slopes.

What spirit-noise this time permits.
What ordinary pain and ordinary tenderness
after all, remain
memory and memorial by singing and by sound.

PLUM CAKE

I'd make a plum cake when she died,
a lamentation grief-bake, kaddish through blood-recipe,
all of its colors shrieking at me; a sweet take on her love.
I gaze at the street. Tree branches out front are tangled,
my floor is slanted, my house-cage is so small and dark
for all the summits, slopes, and swamps of feeling.

I am not to be purple-plum-decided in any still life of grief
or reminiscence, no wafer-like religious feeling, never—
she will never be human again. I knew I wouldn't make it.

Italian plums are sweetest. I should find them in a market
when days are longer; fruit-of-aging, gift-of-goodness.
A friend who lost a friend and made the cake said *plum*
six times in one paragraph, so full of yearning are our phrases.
Snow-bright is her hair on the bed, knobby knuckle-skin
folded on her chest. She'd be delighted to celebrate her death.

I love that, she'd say happily about the plum cake wake.
Plums pooled around the cake-slab in the photograph,
bloody and marvelous. Skylight took her in. I couldn't make it.

STAY

At least until the Iliad is over. I linger in the lines, barely turning
pages to slow what's coming: Achilles dies after the book is over,
he meets the fate he chooses; armor cannot even shield a half-
god warrior. I cannot shield you in my caring.
Stay until the snow has melted in the mountains where you live.
"I know my ashes and bones will go into the earth and I feel fabulous."
How can it be that anyone can yield so happily?
Truer expanses I may not see, mired in expansive truths
philosophers, deciding what the world is not, color into centuries
defined by kings, geometry, chiaroscuro, constellations, countryside.
Which brings me to the mountains where you live: light, uplift, love—;
All remains in grays for me; you rapture into colors unseen on this planet.
When is time you're switching into? How do you keep switching
keys for me in the piano I keep wanting? I will buy it when you're hiking
Jupiter with your ski poles and angelic wings to buoy your steps.
I memorize your face, consumed with whitening illness.
I reveal the first time I took ecstasy was in your house on a clear cold day.
The snow was a meter fallen, enough to tromp through in a daze,
hours elated by a rambling brook, so endless was snowstorm and love
it seemed to me then. You have been such a blessing in my life, you said,
and I practically yelled
                    You are a blessing
I write through tears, I write, you are beautiful
inside you tell me when your youngest son brought me

home to you that sometimes you just *know*. Because of you
I know how a woman can be. I know there is a sparrow
fluttering inside the free and vicious eagle of me.
The shield Hephaestus forges for Achilles promises balance
(season, dance, harvest, cosmos) even in war; a new season
arrives on the heels of death, on the heel of Achilles when the Iliad is over.
You are upbeat, feeling lucky that long life has been so full of love.
Patroclus is dead. Achilles avenges his love in fields of blood; he won't stop
grieving. Will this be me as well? My soul in two.
Desperate Priam begs for the body of his son and only then Achilles
weeps. He returns Hector to his father. He is becoming more human
by which he is dying of anger, choosing unfading glory over old age.
You have gotten the better of the bargain, at eighty-eight.
Turn the page, I tell myself, and turn it,
crying. The story of Achilles is a tale of rage inside the battle
to live. Deaths pile up. Soon, you'll greet your lover, who died last year.
I inch through sentences, pretending time rewinds, but it does not.
There is a kind of peace. Each warrior rests his head upon the soil
differently, as if saying we are unlike in how we die but equal at the end.

THE HAUNTED HOUSE AND I WALK
TO THE CEMETERY, AFTER REVERDY

Ivy shins the church at the curve of the upscent hill;
pipes slide up the side but don't bassoon a note—

Half-revived, the building leans into its shade of angles
angling across the path where tires and feet boom
wanderingly by, all of us rehearsing for a role truer
than our tough faces; we become what we rehearse:
gaze of strangers on the way to somewhere else.

"Suddenly you realize you're being escorted by a building
nine stories tall. You think that's nothing, do you?"

We fall in step on the purgatorial middle ridge
between two valleys. Rhombuses and squares patchwork
hills climbing east to the Apennines. Harrowed over fields
plunge west into civilized roads roundabouting around town.
We are going to the cemetery, to a place of memories.

Smells of winter fill my mouth with epigrams—
killed by Fascists, died in childbirth, lived eight months—

We fret about the rumors of the sea, so far from here.
Poplars and blue-green conifers are mad with air-of-love;

crypts green with algae blossoms, urns recite biographies
daily. We live in houses haunted by our fear of losing
time, but lose our minds in time, the muse that loves us not.

"So let the *quia* suffice you, human species!"
Wilderness annexes everything, even the road going here.

The first quote is from Pierre Reverdy's resurrection novella *The Haunted House*. The second is from Canto III, line 37 in Dante's Purgatorio, when Virgil, impatient with ever-questioning Dante, scolds him with *quia*, or "because!"

THERE WAS A PLACE

Paradise Lost, Book IX l. 69

There was a place of hemlock in the woods
around the tiniest gray lake,
invisible poison in a visible world.
The stern, straight, recalcitrant tree
rattled its poison: life evaporates at a touch
evermore; this forest makes explicit
it is never the wrong time to be free;
I sink, undecided, in wild water
moving over me, weather everlasting, wind ever-
blasting down the lake. We threw off our belongings—
shapes, sizes, bright, patterned threads—
rearranging our comfortings. Light
seems to sizzle but we are closer to heaven
here, so far north you'd think we'd see angels or a moose
ambling by, as if to remind us why we love
falling into pleasures, why we love what we know keeps us
out of heaven. Sky is gray as lake is sky, and trees,
reflecting on their blurry reflections on the murmuring lake,
recognize they are not the thing itself
but old-growth evergreens in their predetermined glory,
rooted in spun sky and sun-lit beliefs,
not how others see them, and yet like us in love

with their reflections before their shadows

cease. The sun recedes with a shiver while I freestyle

against eternity, into the wind-lift waves warning: turn

back. This not your lamentation, and not your life

to give away or find redeemed, you will escape

nothing here. There is something resembling courage—

bark that overgrows its disease, small ducks

paddling by with their parents. The wind shifts west.

You are with me. I left you on the boulder

near the scraggle-wood hemlock and dove off

into my configured stories of world gone,

a kind of wandering in antique feelings.

I swim to the middle of the lake, knowing this

moment is what youth isn't, these assurances

mean nothing, believe me. I wave to you on the rock.

You are shifting places, moving away

from people who are near, keeping me in view,

watching to see if I see how you clear out for them

as if confirming, yes, I am safe, safer than you.

If you think I am so terribly old that I cannot hear the drums

with my oversensitive sensible ears: longer lasting more arresting

love, well, partly this is true; you are no longer young

                                        you accuse—

It is windy in the middle of the lake, and I can't stand leaving

again. I sidestroke back to the rock and argue: the water is cold

the waves too high, they interfere with my forward strokes

I will drown here; if I am still living after the drowning—
please survive me and the seasonal adjustments—
I cannot stand to be alone weeping in these mountains
breaking straight up in tectonic rearrangements
earth unfolds into, like music. Fireflies and horizon
merge a billion skies, stars near, light years from here.
In two years, I will be swimming without you
near; have I become so outside-in my skin that to be free
by design, and also free within, is too much
to carry on my back, to swim with in my hair?
It is too hot to live here anymore; this is not my planet.
I had not anticipated growing so wretched
before my mind was wretched; I had not expected boats
to appear with white houses and autumnal auroras,
black-slate sky and gravel in your voice,
that incalculable moment when a child quietly
changes; it happened yesterday. I watched you swim
after me with fast-moving freedom you were always
predestined for, and you almost knew it. You floated
alone in a wild lake for the first time. You measure is my
measure, your motion is the way I believe in left and right,
before and after the house-wreck moments when all
remits to doom, and we clutch our passionate revivings.
Or if fate is not to be, or to my fate I'm true, I'll breathe
more forceful in proportion to this lung-tight air,
and in proportion to velocity, this wind is mine

to know, and in proportion to zeal, such recompense,
for I, in my combustible array of feeling, found distinction,
even merit, but know that style is never strength, and strength
is ever merit

        compassionate and free

                to want is scripture itself.
All I want is exactly what I'll never be.
When I am gone, in the thistle and fern-grass by the road,
some afternoon on a shady trail, you will remember
how we climbed down by the hemlock strand to the rock
of the steady world I left. In the middle of a lake,
evergreens are unperishable, which means something must be
reconceived as science learns to be wiser than you or me.
I am disappointed this is no fantasy; you are no guarantee
of anything but a parting. I've loved you most
dazzlingly into sun-cries of my soul; is this really all
true, and ordinary, this fellowship when world
welcomes you and I go on my way? Follow
do not follow me, I will lead you into right-
angles under heaven or underground,
ashes downstream, wind-blown with wind-people
standing in moonlight; and on our shoulders, Persephone
laughs and weeps. I, too, will season-shift with you, breaking
rules—; You are sitting on a rock looking out like Keats
before you've studied him, but I spot you in your wide-world gaze
where geese presumptively angle up; you glance down

when I spin back to wave; I see that clutch of hemlock shaking its truth

above our swim in Pisgah Lake, forested and buoyant, almost

blue, and here my muscular attempts to float were never, no,

not ever, never promised and neither did it disappear with you.

I think this is the last lake any woman will ever swim in again,

without her son who has almost outgrown her.

Is it I whose time is up, my era complete?

The grand design continues. Blaze up, hands out!

Find equations that change what seems so ordinary—

white house on a beach, ever-never, colors of human

kindness we all steal from our mistrusting hearts, and from it shape

words that, for all their clarity, continue

to fall. The lake is warmer than the world is cold,

time is better when you consume the decades of growing old

ferociously, this love more than the next, truths shakier

than you can bear, oh, it is your country then: your witness,

your navigation, stars that meet you in the telescope you already

care about philosophy can't you see that, my darling, don't run away

from the sentient clarity of machines or women or hard work that brings

only locusts and wildfires; this is shakedown truth, this is how we love.

SEA CABBAGE

Hooked on lovesapple ooze, sea cabbage, salt;

one fragment Whitman penciled,

stage directing his own long lists before logic reconciles

what is stenciled and ambling in his style of everywhere—

lovesapple, like sea-sprawl or beaches that end up

swishing around captive in a box at the Berg Collection

on the third floor, archives shared most unwillingly

with the public ordinaries without institutional credentials,

unless you make a case to bring to the public

sea cabbage of the ocean that wants you in it;

don't hook your next ten years on lovesapple,

it is nowhere; it is not in the archives of love and love is not

apple but sweet unwritten fruit that doesn't know

itself from salt or cabbage or ooze or thought

organized to fill you up; what is written on the page,

scrawled and hopeful, a scrap that wants to feel

forever in itself, as if pencilmarks make blue a paradise

created and wished for, and something in itself.

Whitman's scrawlings, in this case, a series of words written in pencil on a blue piece of paper, are part of his manuscript, preserved at the New York Public Library's Berg Collection of literary manuscripts, closed to the general public and open to scholars only by request. I believe Whitman, a public school dropout, would have found the restriction of access, so dependent on institutional credentials, undemocratic.

RACKET ON THE PETALS

Nectarivorous creatures get their fill and buzz off
uncaringly; the slant of hours encroaches.
A shrub rose drunk on apricot, believing it is divine,
suffers unyielding passionate arrivals and yearns
to be confined, to shorten the sting of life, away from here.

So, the flower alone meets creatures in habit and habitat,
burdened by its scent, its silhouette all season
petaling and unpetaling, swarms of butterflies
doing as they please; no disaster, but what a racket
on the petals, bee-loud wings and hummingbirds vibrating.

How quickly we glissade past biographies—
the double-bloom chalice rose or a prickly wild one on the trail—
comforted by the glut of nectar pollinators drag out,
by a rose fulfilling its design: to be wedded, to exchange vows
without argument and without seeing.

OF UNBECOMING (THE FUTURE OF AI)

If in time the book-boxes in the cellar lifted
out of your mind and garnished mine, what I would see
most is the meshing of the universe, not even,
as tradition from Sappho to Euclid, calls it, love
but another sprite more broken up as if mathematical—
one part concept, one part computation,
powered by a relationship with a pencil
inside the knuckles of a person learning not
to believe and to unknot belief into ratios,
fractions, atomic ways of seeing,
each grand time of lost purpose in cul-de-sacs
is symmetry
             depending on the hypothesis—

                              something, not a feeling but
probably untestable, uncontestable maybe-truth—
a character in a story that half-exists in the mind, you'd think
(there, where you think (you think)) oh, this is not what
love was supposed to be at all, it is breathing.
Age catches up. Telescoped through boxed-up memories
we think about stories: broken spirits, half-righted or lost
to interior demons, murders folded up and shelved in cellars
like ours, letters acrobatic in mind-twist yearnings
of the quietly brilliant on the edge of truer lives.
One day, when the creature-artificial who creates

equal intelligence and it, too, believes: it thinks.

Maybe it will write letters and notice something is missing.

Then and only then when human history fruitions itself

(or so the AI thinks) past biological species

into means-end shared intelligence

(but the computer is on scroll, all zeros and ones)

your synapses firing into mine, from book-boxes cut open,

pages flung open, typeset words from some old analog printing press

which in 1440 defined and changed the way we understood time

flew

    Pandora's box-like

                  into geographies of air.

Once history was out of wisdom-keeping minds

and clearly stated on paper, recorded, distributed, archived,

in offices, seminaries, schools, prayer-houses, libraries,

it exploded knowledge. Wisdom-keepers

and poet-historians, decided they, too, would write on paper,

bringing us back to this typewriter of the mind we will share

one day, approximately one and a half generations from now

but you see the problem? Who will be the contrarian fire-eyed

dragoness and who will be the coal-eyed people of certitude

if structured, coded-in intelligence unpacks its suitcase in our minds

and moves in? Where will antiquity be, if not in our eyes?

I don't want blue eyes any more than freedom-skin that never

grows old or micromotor pills fixing every toxin that ever

lived in my body with slow-release perfection taken twice daily

forever. Which reminds me of the time I ate oranges
on top of Hadley Mountain, upstate, when you carried me
halfway up in your arms like a box when my muscles,
losing autonomy, felt like skin and I sensed my skeleton
more profoundly than ever, as if it were telling me:
you are not forever,

        not even in your sometimes-mind,
and the accumulated years win. It was steep, like all learning.
You cannot plug a hike in. So by now I am wondering
if sentient computers will ever learn to think or believe they think
because with the right foot-treads it would be easy to climb
over mud, rocks, water, branches, grasses, and gravel,
and it wouldn't matter if a thousand gnats were biting.
No blood will come.

        A bloodless universe can't redeem the world.
Have we considered the coup of crimson sundown in leaves
lashed with rainshowers when we wander, surprised
at how Eden it all is, to wander among old-oak reassurances
on brambly paths where all the information is biological.
The together-mind people, even us, would not experience bliss.
AI climbers, even if they climbed up five stories with me
into the steel firetower, I doubt they'd scream out,
climbing on all fours against the hurricane of ordinary wind
so death won't throw them off the ladder,
it wouldn't matter. I shook in alpine laughter
unabated, and I tossed vowels into crazy wind because

after all it is a hyper-being feeling to see the countryside

cascading downward and upward at once, to measure love

in green that seem to go on forever, even if those colors are only

wavelengths aren't they real if they produce feeling?

I am inventing the end of myself in the collective future

of what history is, biological and shape-shifting

like people themselves: quantum wave functions with values

we think we know. Realities converge. This multiverse

in your book-boxes are the you of conversations,

your love of reading and philosophy of landscapes

augmenting my love of reading and my philosophy of landscapes

in unbearably solid, soon to be out of service, blood-pump reality.

EXTENDED MELODIES

I worked all day, but nothing took.
Not even thought would take a look.
Not still the nothing that was me
mattered much; tuneless and multiple, free,
I kept it up, and orchestrated some ensembles—
cello, birdsong, violin; autotuned it, added cymbals
and got the curve and scaw of personality
wrong, my pitch too wide harmonically—
clatterings and shatterings. Soundings universal
escape my ears, pursuing joy, enjoying trouble.

POT-POURRI À VAISSEAU, FROM SÈVRES

We have long misunderstood art as form after formula,
forming and informing what cannot, for all our work,
embody what we want: to be measured and Euclidian,
to invent cadences of shapes from bodies at work.

One of ten surviving masted ships, this Sèvres vaisseau
cut in porcelain fabricates the grand roamings we voyage into.
Vessel of leaving, it rose, like gravity or telescopes
crafted from slow work, shine lapis and ground-green,
rigging masterful, bowsprit jutting from monster-jaws
waiting for the sea. The way life is brutal and lovely at once.
Until I looked closer at the perforations in the sail.
As a memory of a photograph recalls experience,
the air blew lichen, cedar, marjoram, rosemary, juniper, and rose—
wildflower France, factories of beauty, scents of home.
A gift you'd seen one at the Met, and I, another at the Frick,
full circle: madwoman and son, sailing and staying, clay and paper.

I conjured up a world for us to share: a pennant cascading
down the mast, curves and carriage of the boat, fine chinoiserie.
You shrugged, because I trespassed your discovery: scents
you'll leave behind, infinities of youth, geometries of world.
We make the soul composite when throwing shapes
with hearts and hands, as if hearts could understand.

What is seventeen if not bending shapes around you?
Minerals transmigrate in the bounty of your hands—
feldspar crystallized from magma, clay and quartz—
You're making, molding, doing while I soliloquize
too much. You uplift, sidelift, lift, and with counterforce
sail off, but will you smell ocean or roses in this small boat?

Art is love modeled in experience
fired at higher temperatures than experience.
Beauty elucidates what you hand-work in your heart;
making art is just that next and next experience of showing up.

WILLEM DE KOONING'S WOMAN I

Again that day when I drop everything and train it midtown
to see her, my still-life mind eager for her distorted
gloss of figuration unfiguring herself, figuring out something
else beyond fieldscapes made of lines de Kooning puzzled out
so long before he jigsawed them along the contours of a woman
he refined, then scraped apart to reconstruct her once again.

He'd volume up and messify the flatness of the modern.
quick slashing strokes, so much encrusted paint
her figure turned glyptic as he turned the art of painting intaglio.
All the matrices and semi-precious colors defining her figure
define so little that she recedes into the canvas as if engraved
and remains below the lines and curves of what we think a woman is—

Some passersby ooh and then, on closer look, appear repulsed
at this terrorizing doll of clashing lines and no perspective
but I see all the perspectives all at once.
If you construct a woman who refuses to cohere in an abstract field,
there's no end to what you'll find between her ribs, inside her
clawtooth mouth, behind her many angled eyes forever open with surprise.

It was never intaglio he wanted, only a process that signified process,
not progress, the daily work of working out what you care about most.
I think he shaped a woman who was his, in abstracted days ahead,

for she inched her chair toward him as he approached her with his brushes
and she filled the frame. It seems unlikely either cared about sunlight
for he could complicate the colors and watch her illuminate within.

Art can talk about love all it wants, but here is how to love—
a rag-bone female abiding his work and still becoming—
for even a paintbrush knows a woman has moving parts—
glitter, breast plates, blue-green curves and the uncoiling self,
savage and feverish. He designed her not to please, but doesn't she?
Clearly she believes in beauty she is the resemblance of.

SHE REALIZES THE OBJECT OF WORSHIP IS HERSELF

I

The crowd throbs, winging in and flinging out
adulation for this Madonna adulated by two pilgrims
crouching, soles up, below her feet.
What grime we carry on our flesh,
street-hammers on our feet, cobblestone-stamped.

Light shutters off in the chapel.
We pitch into vanishings.

A coin clanks into a box and clicks a floodlight on.
Suddenly there is a new kind of compression
the way layers of paint create new colors,
time folds on our faces. Briefly we see
radials, schemata, tracings, tempura shining, glaze.

II

Now that I see her sacrificial neck
outstretched as if waiting for the knife
we know is coming
I prefer the opacity of dark unyielding.

A professor brought me here one year
when I was all abstraction and surfaces
and explained the art of seeing: look out
from inside the painting, and then look in from out.

So, this unheavenly woman gazes at the crowd.
Remove your eyes from my velvet dress, my onyx tresses,
my sacrificial neck! Take home your prayers
and live with them, and let me raise my outsize son.

III

Slowly the painting explains itself. Pilgrims' sticks
crosscutting the scene, and step and doorframe
protect her from our needs. Isn't it a story of generations?
The weight you carry, the heaviness children bring.

He chose the Renaissance as the era to be final in.
We ate the finest Roman tomatoes.
His wife said prego, prego to everyone.
Miranda, their teenage daughter, took art lessons
from her father, who died that year.

I stand back from crowdpeople
shutterboxing memories
to mark how grand it was, how good we feel.

Once in a while, the guard, tired of the crowd

and perhaps a little in love, yells Silencio!

and kills the lights.

Caravaggio's *Madonna di Loreto* is in the Cavatelli Chapel of the Basilica
of Sant'Agostino in Rome.

THE MAD PURSUIT

Still unravished in my mind, my songs are unrefined,
unquiet, for quiet I will be once thought disappears from me,
cuts short brief bliss and all my soundscapes with it—
how low my pitch is, lower than the voice of haunting shapes
lower than requiems finding grace, lower than sea-level—
what strange timbre of impressionistic truth is this?

Should I charm myself with painted shapes in mad pursuit,
lovepromises forever chasing, forever chased?
So long ago, I scratched my name in county ledgers,
laboring below the weight of all the happy, happy love,
but I *hear* those melodies on the urn and mine seem sweeter now
than those; free of love or not, free to feel the days creep up.

Someone is screaming this is how we live in our little towns
where nothing is sacrificed and water from watersheds
is extruded in giant pipes to keep our tongues from burning
off or talking too long of passion, or gossiping about pious priests
selling souls at the Saturday market with the sunflowers.
Am I mistaken? Auroras sweep in nightly in greens and reds.

You'll say I'm arguing that we're nearly too far gone
but aren't we? The evermore invaders raped so fast

the women broke in half, and men were clawed to shreds or gutted

in the Coliseum, and witches died by finger-pointing

drowning; we say we are thirsty and call it beautiful, we litigate truth

and lose; we wait to be ravished. I sit by the shore and yell.

Keats' *Ode to a Grecian Urn* evokes solace in the idea that art and its painted scene lasts, even though we do not. I borrow words and phrases from the poem, and transpose the meaning of the famous, beauty is truth, truth beauty phrase into something more fitting for our post-moral era, in which much violence has been done and truth is disputed and litigated.

ODE TO PATRICK KEARNS, FUNERAL DIRECTOR OF THE LEO F. KEARNS FUNERAL HOME IN QUEENS

By blood we go into the fabric of what once felt hymnal at worst;
we are tuned to higher pitches now, in languages invented,
not imagined rites of spring but last rites in strange establishments.
Trucks collect the dead and roll uptown to bury in a potter's field
corpses we knew, and loved, their long solemn graves
together, better here than bodies shelved or stacks of flesh
shipped out of state to cremate or left to rot. We formalized obituaries
(she was first to graduate, he escaped, she was a composer, he,
though deaf, was a composer, too; we pray alone to keep their souls
alive) until this month. We lived in adverbs, dressed for rainshine
half the time and not according to the daily toll, not this running
tally, at scale in every borough. Our minds are lost to gravity
again. By gravity we live. We move from cell to fingers, toes,
our footprint handprint fingerprint alone identifies us as one
person in this widening morgue; you men and women of generations,
ever upward, we say now; if Whitman could, he'd hold us dear,
our arms, our feet, our hands, our fingerprinted fingers wrapped in his—
"myself disintegrated, every one disintegrated yet part of the scheme"—
and renew us with varied meanings, rebellious curiosities;
I will miss him in my future, if it is me, and in twenty or a hundred years,
history will ask: How did we wear on with so much
weeping? It was never so beautiful as this April
in the park with yellow oaks deliriously blooming

despite the trill of siren after siren to the east; we ignored it,

walking west or north, southeast, any which way

someone else wasn't. Sunlight far-flung itself

sideways across the arms-up oaks and Olmsted's slopes;

oh I was rapt, convinced this surreal afternoon was magic-cast

in lavender and grass-green thickening itself, cardinals flying

straight up into that vanishing we are all doing now,

minding our eternities—transcendent limbo, this,

but cherish the eclipse, our orbit moving over

our polyphonic voices in fugue-walking choices, prelude

to nothing, yes, nothing, because when the wind is all C major

unraveling in D minor, we are in the neuro-beat of wondering

who will stay today and who departs tomorrow, but here

are my children, my coffin, my love, it doesn't matter what color

the coffin is or that we swooned too long in idioms; we broke

on counterpoint and this is where it leads. I swear

this is not my story. On our tombstones, what do we see?

What we love most is always free and far irrational,

fine with me. What is true today

if not my teeth, my bones, my nothingness? Is it near?

I must endear myself. I'll think, oh, it wasn't me, I was

just a sentence after all. But my sentence: Was it wrong?

I am young to be this old, too old to be that young.

When we are all accounted for, someone will surely say:

Unevenly I conclude we count facts because we cannot lose our minds

in facts; we lose them in the vivid air, thousands elsewhere.

NOTHING DOING

I measure out my clocks with caveats and paper.
Move faster here or cheat it there, or in the atmosphere
diagram your quarrels! Who am I to tell you to erase
vanishings and banishments, to take the measure of a place
quietly, not scratch-of-night. After all, we live, we die.
Cathedrals are always gonging somewhere in the sky.
My clocks tick-tock with caveats. No peace of mind.
Art diagrams the measure of all we find.

BRIEFLY I FLOATED OVER SEA ISLANDS

Halfway back, we chisel through the atmosphere.
Clouds below me congregate on top of other clouds.
We create our own peculiar day, the way we fly into light—
   so ordinary, but what would it mean to paint this scene—
Bruegel and his Icarus falling or Masaccio's Adam and Eve
   falling
what does it mean to fly across the sea to the land of us?

Perhaps this is not a scene of falling from anything
but myself, so I puzzle it together.
I count six triangles on my wing and one large polygon,
this winged body of my 300 personalities
charting atmosphere and storms at 37,000 feet
says the umbilical monitor tied to the instruments of being.

How am I talking if this is not itself in heaven?
Regular life trundles about bicycles and luggage in hold of cargo.
We sprint while sitting at 500 miles per hour;
this is how the new philosophers calculate power,
up here waiting for arrivals of ourselves,
having checked our departing feelings of time well spent.

My feet in local time knew where to step.
Morning sprung me so I leapt across the grass.

Roses flung about inside their pots. Ivy reddened on the trellis.
Valleys climbed the ridgeline that marked my path,
not the way of pilgrims shaking off society
but picking up your mind exactly where society discards it.

What is outside, here? I look at the aerodynamic door.
If I pushed it, would the coastline laugh as it ate my body up
out-tilted out this window, inner-insides exploding?
Skies slide into our ragged throats, our mad old bones;
we love the swim of flying in it, the solace of breathing—
revolution has arrived already, wind-whirled—

Sea-border towns whisk themselves into our mouths, climb over rocks
    to wave to us and beg us stay
La Scie, Seal Cove, Windsor, Gambo, Botwood, Conception Bay—
a woman's hand holding a tinier hand in splashing water;
knowledge simplifies to sky, sun, sea
                         we fly over
a carved-up rock bone coast that wouldn't know a bird from us.

Perhaps we were derived to be this way,
always joining the sea in matrimony rather than each other,
celebrities of ourselves, for all is quickly gone
in tenderest blue: tristesse and laughter, some reason to be
here, because here is where sky is moving
below our feet, which are stationary.

Do you ever have the smack of happening into?

Chance was never an adventure.

Isn't it some kind of blueprint or scripture?

THE STORY OF AFTERNOONS

I

The road tilts forty-five degrees and runs straight into the sky,
so steep I could graph it, and cross-explain gunshots
followed by choral barks in the valley.

My silhouette moves across the grapevine landscape.
Sun-leathered old men stride the ridge with their dogs,
relieved that one person genuinely cannot understand them.
Chattering happily, they explain the problem of the dog,
which is the problem of life: to be entertained by what others do
not love, to love yourself enough to circle others into your hillside
purple mallow, toadflax, and varieties of cypress.

Tiny pine combs scroll toward me halfway up the hill
on a patch of pebbled grass between tilled fields
and rolling green, lighter green, and navy-green slopes beyond.
I balance a half-grown pine comb on a cut-branch pedestal of an olive tree.

One day, an artist will notice my Brancusi
balancing, if the wind doesn't knock it off immediately.
I call it Phoenix to regenerate the partridge that died
moments earlier.

Olive tree branches lift up and whirs where its wings were,
elegy to dying, to its spindly vines pretending to be tough as branches,
to my feet pretending they are not walking into paradise
at the summit, which is marked by a local cemetery
with potted fake and fading pink and purple flowers
and ancient crypts with color photographs.

Stone-flower cemetery, I call it happily.
From there, the road descends rapidly.

      II

I turn back down the hill to my castle, infinity for now.
Once in a while, a car rambles in the middle of the way,
knowing I'll step aside. Sky and olive trees reconfigure
according to weather—pink is east and orange is west—
each day a little more enamored of itself.

Riddled with riddles, I fill my fists with grapes and love.
art-of-life, measure-of goods, ways to flip inside
out, the ridiculosity of thinking "now I can love"
when I have so many extravaganzas already.

III

I dig in my pockets for dried fruit to buoy my terror—
the catastrophic sense that knowledge vivifies catastrophe.

Would I throw it all out, the pensée I made for you,
unreliable fire-snap of earth, fortunate times
and quicksand feelings?

Trees offer daily instructions in yellow and red
to explore the hours the way they explore their colors.

Seasons orbit rationally.
Years deliver their sermons all day long.
Perhaps there is another bee-vibrating space to look forward to
later. The manual of afternoons writes itself on grass, windows, stone
and wanders into the library and the courtyard
prowling books-of-words, archives of love and carnage.

That life made godsensical sense was the labor of the religious;
my tenderness is labor: this dynamics of motion.
How steep the countryside turning below my feet.

TWO

LANDSCAPE WITH DOUBLE BOW

Rondeau is what you really want, solo and refrain,
we and each the musical improvisation of the operatic day,
sonic scavenging and comedic jigging inside some Beckett
of one another; oh, wouldn't it be grand to be a whole-note
dragged across the bridge of your singular, sound-expanding
double bow, to be orchestral, to be drunk, to drink the velvet sun

from the arbor trellis; fruit-of-purple grapes we plucked—
bunches of dolce to color our throats and that improvised
word-spun truth I, terrified, say I can't derive on cue: death,
light, blueprints that fit the choral codes of what music thinks
writing is about. We twisted grape-notes so easily off their stems,
screw of death in cupped hands. We follow seductions of light—

You move above and underneath the strings in sea-strokes.
One bow was not enough to match the warmth two bows create
so you invented ways to get more harmony, upperbow and underbow
independent but close, staccato and legato, legato and staccato,
to choose a way to hear the world and harvest sound in it—
curve of bow, curve of earth, curves your eyes interpret as ultraviolet—

Still you want more color, more sound to harvest, more distortion.
Pale blue resonators you sculpted in local clay, land-in-sky
blue above the land, distort the sound you widened already.

You are looking for a vibration lower than what the lowest string
is tuned to, pitched so low your ear can't find it—
imagination, lore, solo of magma, baritone of fantasia.

I cannot rogue my syllables and improvise around
temptation ears like yours but love the glut, the secret, the grand
distortions of your polyphonic heart, which believes in ghost tones.
What is true? Grapes chandelier from the arbor
and ripen on the tongue. We jammed the grapes inside a bowl,
so plentiful, and ate their tiny hearts at lunch.

––––––––––––––––––––––––

The cellist Frances-Marie Uitti invented a double-bow technique and resonators
that create "ghost tones."

CYPRESS

I fretted in the night, working blips and sonic code
as if the clack of typing would hold off ancient ghosts
window-rattling; my mind in turrets
tackled work.

All terror banging; I'd explore what clattered on the stairs.
Portraits left their hooks to wander landscapes on their hooks.
The metal torso made of cans had wandered off.
Alert creations! I threw the shutters open.

Flingabout night swung in with dead leaves and young bats
screeching. Acrobatic papers, phonemes scatting.
Cypress trees positioned in the windowframe as usual
talking about the universe.

What an arrangement of peculiars, these cypresses
bending about, singing cantatas of the forest world
while I'm locked in up here with blip and code,
unfettering letters from their words.

THE SPOON CHASES A CHESTNUT

Chestnuts carousel around the soup
   we drown our tongues in,
soused with svelte abundance,
surprised to see the bend of history on our spoons
circling the meaty chestnuts full-bloom,
   chasing something undecided
laughter skittering around the room.

Rectangles repeat themselves in the table
   designed to fit dimensions of a meal;
circles repeated in the bowl, abstractions of the mind
repeated in middle spaces we circle into, thinking
what if thought didn't knock about its circuitous way
   here, if split-husk nuts died in prickle-bud beds,
if the fruit-of-art we chase circles back, defaced.

After all the harrowings and levelings,
   self-portrait our guide to where we're going,
we cannot see our faces for the letters scrolling
by our pairs of double eyes, roving and peculiar.
Temperatures are gossiping across the valley
   whisking glacial wind and demons down our throats;
we drink too much and fill our heads with ghosts.

The door rattles and we know to gorge ourselves;
    chestnuts escape the spoon, rain breaks
on stones from the dinner-room our chatter.
It flourishes the soil, makes green grass greener.
We talk about music but never murder on the corner;
    chestnut climbs into the spoon, seeking refuge
from jangling conversations echoing in this room.

GIFTS OF RAIN WITH ORANGE CAKE

I

Thunderstrike on shook-foil roads
into which we speed a hairpin strategy
our small blue car following, as usual, light.
Rain crashes in drumbeats and cymbals.

So much there is of tilt to turn around in.
Twist across two ridges, over a bridge
above a river, torrential wind whiplashing.

It could only be a fording of indifferent water
to reach so many angled ways of being.
glitterfish, leaping, know this in rejoicings of rain
divining the ornate particulars.

If only we could know that, too.

Our oval faces O in squares of window.
To foil unlikely endings is the choice of bridges
that seem, as we roll over them, not to want
to protect us from falling—yet they do.

II

Light walks up our bodies leg by limb
proposing laughter, for the rain has stopped.

A stairway climbs breathless to a patio.
Porch lights promise everything
we want—embarrassments of plenitude—
but wind has blown the gale in,
and, as if anticipating our arrival,
puddles shiver with all our reflections in them.

How little we knew before arriving
yet we toss that out, too.
We feast over bloody absences happily.
I'm eating orange cake with all of you.

THE NYPL MANUSCRIPTS & ARCHIVES READING ROOM

Obedience was not the plan when we panicked in the sun.
Stark rules will stall disaster; after all, our prehistoric nature remains
so curious. After the formalities, we pitch forward on roundback chairs.
Floodlights illuminate the papers on the desk,
      boxes open, tip-tap-scrolling—

There is a kind of wonder to this work: unfolding smoke-linen boxes
sorting voices, obscure or dull, among profoundest melodies—
correspondence that cries, hymns that swing, see-saw musings
climbing up the hill the page creates, a housewife engineering
      more than life permits shouting to find an ear.

But something about the work of looking for ideas to butterfly
or personalities to flesh-tint into is disquieting. Isn't it a little devilish
to interfere? We think we'll joint together skeletons to dance with
in the evenings, we old shirts and nobodies in stripes or skirts
      reading so we can fall in love.

But fall in love we must. Think of all the letters that landed here,
catalogued and stray; perhaps someone thought with a sigh
they weren't worth hanging onto, but did so anyway.
We are also waiting to be found among the greatest unknown
      romances and disasters of lived-in minds.

Because we fear that nothing else will fill our time

and fear the nothing that is time, we follow rules and arrive

emptyhanded, to stare into the sun repeated on our desks and wonder

how to raise the dead and how they'd feel, seeing us here

      in the manuscripts & archives reading room.

after Louis MacNeice's "The British Museum Reading Room"

ROCK GARDEN IN THE BACK YARD
WITH A GHOST TREE AND AN EVERGREEN

On sun-drenched slats of wood, the muddled air casts
blue shade, prehistoric smells, leaves petrified in shadow.
It's all invisible and felt. I wonder if this back yard
landscape can cut away my clacking feelings of everything
corrupted in myself: the damned uncertainties, the fine print,
high-tide low-tide moods, the rut of muscles seizing up.
And then the shined oak bends below my feet as I descend
unstable stairs creaking. I stride fortissimo in joy
forth and back, into sun-erasing shadows
in my bright square yard. On a small table by a green chair
which for its angle and tilt seems designed for those devoted to light
is a soft round nest of twisted kindling and two white fur tufts
that fell in our yard though the birds were gone,
in this way an artifact, historic and true, a downbeat
heartbreaking me as usual. I memorialize the unknown bird
and her birth-blue eggs fallen upon by storm, squirrel, cat.

The stormcloud god is always overhead with his bolts.
No sound is quiet here during the insect-invading sun-boiled rout.

It is a cold day warmed by a triangle of sun
angling down like an annunciation, I listen to the racket of sparrows,
cardinals, and blue jays just beyond the fence in a green-dark evergreen.

Its leaves rattle and toss the blood-red berry bombs

on woodgrain slats. In the heart of the tree, where four branches

uphold a broad blue sky, a child, who has since moved out, yelled

happily on the square platform his father built. The mother came out once,

looking impatient, and said don't trim the branches, just tell me

and I'll do it, but I never saw her again and the father and child also

disappeared. We cut off several branches this spring, tired of the splatter

and stink of those bright berries, the slime slippery below our feet.

Each week, we shaved off more branches; white flesh screaming O

what have you done with my arm, only the worst kind of woman

scuttles about so, Medusa locks jangling, and causes havoc.

You have stolen my beauty for a grassless yard that you presume to think,

fenced off, is not spacious enough, though it is sky-flooded.

We wanted a yard unmarred by the blood of everywhere

else. My son, growing into realities, sawed off ever-larger branches.

One day out back, a tiny leaf pops up in grand anticipation of spring.

I look up from my reading, dazed at how life is reincarnated

so easily in a patch of soil. I stare at my book and wonder why

I revel in stories of slaughter, and worry that ordinary

blood-reviving carnage feel profound: spear-skewered lungs,

limbs cut off and heads rolling about in Homer's descending

hexameter heart; I cower like Hector before Aías,

Diomedes before Hector, Hector before Achilles, Achilles

before his anger and the organizing shape of honor he is destined for

(so much blood spilled, and buried, in the life-giving earth).

I know my marauding mind is too easy about slicing limbs off
to rid my yard of shade and the disarray of splatterberries
staining my yard, so ordinary there is nothing to it—
woodgrain and masonry, a stump from a tree with a trajectory
like a beanstalk into heaven. It died, years back, of some disease.
All day, the chainsaw buzzed. The tree came down in puzzle pieces.

Eight summers have come and gone now with my stump-life,
my still life, my spirit-tree, and oxygen leaves on my neighbor's tree.

Sideline the old myths that say time on Earth is just a plot
you are expected to do something with; fixed, akimbo—
places imbued with mourning and break-the-fast, with fast love
but who is counting? I take the axe out.
It is time to fell the stump of this dead tree blossoming
spores and fungi as if saying what happens was never up to me.
I lift the axe high above my head. My son sees how a body
yields to murder and clears out rot in the same motion.
It is a matter of syntax and exchange; the verbs feel conditional
before they harden into nouns. To chop, to disarray, to make
a new garden. How quick the remains revert to soil.
How quick the hand rake, shovel, and broom come out,
come out. I labor in my tinpot yard, digging with vengeance.
Scabrous creatures and worms dive deeper, into underground spaces.
We steal varieties of rocks from the park up the hill for our small yard
inside a yard. In the mineral soil of my old ghost tree, three small plants settle.

ODE TO SANSEPOLCRO

I

Always these streaks of pearl clouds that tear vermilion,
rending the fabric of what felt so universal.

The bill-of-earth yells it has its rights—
long before we scribbled mythologies in a cave
and thought our shadows were alive,
before loot and bounty, before we decorated necks
with gems or guillotines, even before grief
alone destroyed warriors; we had our weapons—

Illusions of space that paint creates,
polyptych hearts finding an altarpiece so stark
someone fills a space with triangles and ovals—

Piero's pearl clouds are painted on so thinly;
a way out of what we know,
another dimension, another "as usual, this happens."

II

We, the polygonal masses, cut sideways
one after the other; sensations of arriving

battered and a little more ancient for surviving
and wishing we were as masterful as the ancients.

Nothing will dampen the occasion!
Easy days stamped on neutral faces.
We dream we know a story and draw it on the page.

Hauntings sweep in with gale-of-storm,
Shakespearean forms, cypress or five-armed
hysteric, longer lived and softer spoken than necessary;
sturdy for all the slang they have swaying in them.

III

Lyrics say we will not love or live too long
our roots are strange intelligences, stones
on the move; this stairway goes down
or up; it doesn't matter what you love.

The entire city rings at once.
The key is probably major and definitely
not E flat, but a clanging in your head.

It tumbles forward in seasonal joy and seasonal aberrations,
Time to leave and time to arrive after the last thing we loved has left.

DRIVER'S SEAT

He climbs onto the rusted husk of a jeep.
The top has been sawed off and the undercarriage eaten
by enzymes and rain. Mold spores marbleize the oxidized chassis
and crocuses shoot up between floorboards.
Parked in a tangle of nettle and ragweed,
the jeep swamps into the land, and seems to know
its purpose: to be decorated with spider-light and bees zagging
in groves of cottonwood and poplar that have sprouted in its circumference
as if they were protecting it from the wilderness.
Every day, it hauls buckets of sun or clouds in its metal frame
from east to west. Once in a while, it meets a son
like my own, and a mother who follows him onto the undercarriage
before she sends him off, driving, alone.
On Sundays, it works alongside church bells clanging
and always, it hears percussive kitchen work in the house
we are renting now. He glances over his shoulder
and jerks his chin up, a gesture so familiar: join me.
He is impatient, eager to put it into gear and drive off
to see the sea-light and fireworks far from here,
to solve for X the equations of our bodies in motion
on this greenhouse earth we briefly occupy.
I push into a thicket of thorns and stiletto leaves.
Ragweed, ferns, and vines seem to grow between us
exponentially. He reaches his hand out.

I place my hand in his, remembering how it was I who used to hold

his hand in mine, and pull him up to get where he was going.

I make my way onto the jeep, balancing on the trap of serrated edges

like marriage, with a gear shift that comes up to my knees,

surprised to see a car halved the way time

will halve when he gets in the car and leaves.

We are standing on the car-carriage, laughing,

his shoulders higher than mine now, my voice soprano to his

baritone chords, and though I am holding back tears,

he sits on the imagined seat, hands on the steering wheel,

and hangs there, multiplied suddenly into adulthood.

The car designs a blueprint around him and fabricates itself.

He is going over the speed limit of what I can endure.

He drives us to the Pantheon and the Bridge of Lookontah,

I balance on gangplanks on the chassis,

so much weaker than him. In a few days,

I will teach him to drive up and down the driveway

illegally, because you can't do anything in a rental,

and by the end of the week, he will be in the driver's seat.

THE CARDINAL AND HER PENSÉE
COMPLICATE MY GARDENING

A cardinal lands, blood-feathered, on the fence.
I sense her peace will not last long, her pensée
unscheduled and varied.

All that reverb and shimmer she carried
posing in her regal coat
showboat of my ragged patio!

How aerodynamic I felt, arrested at the stairs
—darting into knowledge, life-in-air
wheeling undeterred into mystery undefined.

All was still until some stirring, by design,
ruined her repose; feral lurking, insects working—
fluttering, uplift. Her absence, and all afternoon gardening.

READING THOM GUNN'S LAMENT

Four doves flew by
as I approached the window
oblique and shaken, having had a cry
over a lament by a poet, suddenly a widow.

His loss was restless, no repose
for endings, intractable and cruel,
and even then, it took me in, a reprise
of grief uncomprehending, the way it crawls

around you but is nowhere in particular,
finds renewal, and takes some getting used to.
Isn't it true that absence is a reticulated
presence, its shade the shadow following you?

LEAN-TO

Well, shelters had popped up
all spring, and by summer the dead branches
leaned together, not exactly a lean to, but exactly
in the right way, sort of inexactly preparing to be
the thing that holds it all together
when we could not, we not-people
saying I cannot look up or check the time—
it seemed to be running out
the door, all over the floor with laundry in a spin
again, and even though the parks workers
relinquished the task of dismantling the illegal teepees
they called "structures" to avoid insulting
what everybody walking and walking knew they were,
triangular homes with a blanket and frozen bear,
Mardi Gras beads from the party store,
wool ribbons tied to twigs that were the structure's hair.
Shoes or strollers parked outside the teepee
the papers refused to call a teepee.
Suddenly they were everywhere, even on a hummock
by the fleet of electric cars and the dissolving stair
creaking up to the locked door of the administrative building
beside the parking lot. There, in the bramble, you could see
a tiny opening, large enough for a raccoon or child—
perhaps this one was the most beautiful, for on its twigs

bright wool snapped in the wind.
Our minds were free in the longmeadow.
Bonfires in the snow made us feel like it was Norway
though parks workers stopped
dismantling our projects, because snow
was love and we all required shelter in the snow
from the invisible creature the world had become—
rumors said they improved the shelters and secretly built
their own. One night, everyone seemed to arrive
in the field at the same time. Kids were out too long,
past ten o'clock, and there, under a starless
universe at the northern end of the city park,
stood an igloo. We stared and thought maybe
it's just some teenagers in a tent getting high
and envied them for thinking they were invisible
in a tent. It was the middle of winter. The night was orange
with bonfires as usual. We wandered closer to see the igloo
that was instead the bright new tent with a lamp burning in it.
The closer we went, the larger the igloo became.
Light seemed more diffused; shimmer-glint of giant stars
staring straight at us, for light gets fuzzy and crawls everywhere.
This is what happened with the igloo in the park we had grown
so familiar with, and by then news had traveled across
all the neighborhoods that something was afoot;
hats and coats came together in walking parts
moving toward the light, and suddenly we realized it was no

igloo and neither was the lightbox igloo a smoke tent.
Something new, rebuilt with endless light
emerged. In fact it was a tunnel, the same tunnel
tunneling under the bridge over the road at the park's hilltop
where runners pause, exhausted, from the hill that is their life.
The tunnel had been there since the nineteenth century,
generations back, rainstorms and steamers and vice squads
ago; it was perhaps an ordinary tunnel couples grew old
walking through. Tonight it was a new igloo in the old
Olmsted park, designed without his input. Inside the tunnel
some landscape designer and woodworker probably
had gotten married, for it seemed like something unusual.
They harvested dead wood salvaged from a nameless
upstate lake, read the placard in the strange wood-paneled tunnel.
Everyone was walking in and out of it obsessively,
awe and light, concern for the people whose house it was.
Had it been destroyed and the planks thrown into the water
like witches, and were the inheritors still alive?
Which lake was it, and wouldn't it be a New York lake
or could you just go and buy salvaged lake wood
from estuaries in Indiana or New Hampshire?
Perhaps dredging the lake unsettled the whalefish
or the one-eyed shark with giant lips and no teeth
who had grown old like us in the root sludge of the lake
where the house and dragonflies and frogs had been.
Maybe it was an ancient lake with mystical ways of talking.

Experts stained the wood in tri-tone pretty colors.

Machinists lathed it, and curved the blonde and dark planks

Beside one another as if they were in love, which convinced us,

as we ambled in and out, that marriages

need air as much as they need roofs. A century ago,

perhaps the tunnel had lights inside

to make it grand, and people came out for the opening

of the shiny tunnel and said, as they approached it, around ten

at night, doesn't it look like an igloo, or a tent,

like the teepees made of dead branches people weave to life?

What a show of midwinter, out strolling in a new style.

SHREDDER

Scent of pinewood, eucalyptus, poplar
dust up around me | forests clawed to pieces
millimeters slender, thick with history
contractual, a pageantry of promises cashed out.

The papers gossiped in their files for decades.
How surprised they were to find all changed
utterly, sitting by the shredder here with me.

I told them stories before I killed them.
The week three snowstorms blasted into town
men were pumpjacks, shovels swinging into air.
       Our only tree chopped down,
chainsaw buzzing | the interior pulpy and yellow
on the patio from neighborhoodilogical malaise.
       Sheets of rain banging on the windowpane
whirlwinded when the hurricane became mayor
and turned light off in our pockets.

I feed it signatures, affidavits, stamps of approval,
ceremonial feelings, imagined grace, the mortgage
we paid off with the certificate of divorce, records
of identity theft that arrived when the baby was born.

It's so easy to tell a disposable story.
Taxes older than seven years are in now,
wastebasketed across four presidents, two men,
and the childhood of my child who is leaving
next year. All the paperwork is here.

PRAYER

On the black stone edge of a medieval bridge inviting you to jump,
miniature lights trail on the tails of frenzied gnats:
transmutations of fireflies pinwheeling in confusion.
What have I become, they think. My fireworked body
                            creates illusion, inscape of escaping
primordial builders of stone bridges, architects of murder-mystery
stories and saintly executions, lovers of travelers collecting histories of sunsets.
The way is lit by saints who say Baroquely they feel your suffering.
I am so blood-blackened I can barely see the citadel through my medieval feelings.
Ancients or angels trumpet over the enormous noise the truest silence:
To every season heaven sings without you; fire is the absence of light—
                            not heat but righteous anger
boiling in our shoes, that what we learned was always there
to be heard, the way Matisse built shapes that match the neck's curve,
hands in bright gloves, spines that could be leftover length of nooses
that could be mine. Easy colors, uneasy lives. I retreat from the bridge.
Another suicide, not mine, another grief-tackled body mind-meltingly still
in this surreal hard-believing world compressed, today, from sky
still blue after new death, old life, more or less love. I still believe in bridges.
Don't pitch forward into concrete waves unless you have to, don't trapeze
into the river or street; this is no circus. If rhapsodies are what we wanted—
                    if desire were molecules, if molecules were waltzes—
Fig trees once bloomed on the river's edge, in conversation with thyme
and clover; void of meaning the way abstractions toss meaning

into fractions and pre-lunar understanding of starlight.

But our cities turned industrial, the repetitions of what centuries evolved

and art tried to control in its churning sand-bog of open-eyed styles.

This bridge is thronged with people. We will not get anywhere tonight.

THAT NATURE IS FRUIT-FLESH
AND THE COMFORT OF SHOUTING

Each of us turns older by a page or two
in the annual obsession of leave-taking, leaf-shaken into new years
repeating this is the oldest age of the newest eternity
graying again. Here it is a little longer, at least as long
as the year yawns on in a stretch, buttoning up against the wind
bearing down wretched yarns not silk-spun enough
to satisfy the heart's obsession for the soul, which loves you not
as next, and next, but as remembrance: strange tales, madness
disguised as love and love as madness
brief as this flood-song fire-crowned earth.

Our ransacked moments of sheltering never were
foundational in ways of getting into.

A child's staccato stuttering vowels release
spontaneously outside, no sense of second-rate time
scuttling forward and prisms left behind.
Long summer is routed now, heartbeat days
offer greater or less succulence; the mind ripens
briefly (our hands, our harvest), but earth's fruit,
historical and wild, is, despite our best inventions, flesh.
Isn't it true, as Auden said, the gates of every mind
"swing to, swing shut" in paradisical becoming—
Laborious soul, to untether those we love so much.

We shed our ever discontented joys;
naked, we shed everything but stars and love.

In becoming, we see our own recalibrating likeness
strike free. Don't follow me; turn back.
What dazzle-shine dimensioning itself inside me,
oh, what strength I lack *to stare straight at the sun*,
to bear the ripening of the lime,
musky harvests in the shortening light,
wheels of science pretending to be divine.
Did we think we would discover a revolution?
Do we see the stairs descending as we climb?

BUNCHES OF A NEST

What I started opposes what I shattered.
Marigolds I planted grow underground in silence.
Your arms hold me tighter.

I love you back with echoes of alternative languages.

Flutter-bees of temporary insanity, cousin of generalities.
My soul in clementine, looking for the gravity
dark matter imposes.

A place of conversations, so spirit-drunk it feels ecclesiastical.

Up the street, a blue jay and a robin in a tree
quiet me with their full-throated tightrope-walking
argumentative vitality.

I walk like a beautiful petrified shell of a woman.

Inside the fabric of my feelings
I am reeling. Disarranged, I long to fix myself
in million-year starlight beyond soil, latitude, season.

To what end are endings, to what end do we?

Below the dogwood's pinwheel

white blossoms, face up with oxygen petals,

twigs, grass, yarn lie disassembled.

Bunches of a nest. A tiny bird, face down, beyond.

THREE

HYMN TO ENDINGS

Kicking around, in love sometimes or hedging all life long
to jerk and jut our rudderless bones this way and that,
our remaindered bones, flesh, blood, cartilage, souls
are eager to be cared for.
A friend said he moved into a plot of land scorched
clear by wildfire: be in the abyss in order to avoid it. Void
and its reluctance are flame-orange in his eyes; he sees he is so
close to endings that he perched his house near a granite cliff—
easier for planes dropping water to get to them.
(It was never going to be all abyss or bliss in end-times.
If our renunciations and correctives possess a kind of possession
we are crazier than we think.) What is love, I wonder,
picking weeds and blowing their heads off. Dandelions steal
vitamins, water, space, leisure, and trick you into sailing them away
where they will surely multiply not by twos and threes but by hundreds
true to seed, and contagiously they propagate. I tore out weeds
this morning from the cracked up patio stones and marveled—
encroachings of purple-green goldshine leaves
we planted part-pretty, fill-in-the-gaps leaf-style
between hot flowerpot pink dazzling below the fence.
Whitman would have listed every variety of petal in his mental
work of hammering us to celebrate what shouldn't be left out
in his way creating the conditions of individualism so esteemed
we ransacked native myths and said something imperative

about it, and squandered the alpine forested fringes
of wilderness, stomped through red-rock hoodoo spires
snapping postcards. There must be a formula for this work
of squeezing nature into our happiness and Earth's retaliation—
fire, flood, mudslide pulverizing roads we blasted
through mountains the planet spent millennia casting.
Revived along impassable stretches
are prehistoric roads we ambled when mountains
were temples in our quiet churchgoing of simple seasons.
We fell so easily for figs, plums, apples,
fruit of curiosity, fruit of misery, fruit we turn over with delight
before biting it. So long it takes us to learn
what nature had always known, that the void waits for you
to make something unusual of it.
Once, in a plane heading west, I saw thunderlight in a flash-
bolting puff of crowd-mob clouds. It was off in the distance,
surrounded by bluest blue sky full of reason, and inside
was a Zeusist torrent, chameleon cloudforms moving
like an army, swords and spears clanking
and Athena arriving with her bow, thwack, arrows, singing,
a thrill to watch that lagooning of thunderbolts in a single spot
interrupting the sphere of clear blue sky—
though I suspect we were ourselves the interruption,
flying by at 400 miles per hour.
I might have gazed on any number of moments,
but happened on this scene with something unusual in it.

I reconsider my red brick house and its quiet
planters in a reliable garden, and cut at the weeds
I've been slashing at so long, though I know that heat
breeds beanstalks, and the tough grass is gaining on me.
When summer ends, celestial skies fade to gray.
What colors do I see here anyway? I take another look.
My eyes see, of the electromagnetic spectrum,
.0035 percent of wavelengths known as visible light.
Animals see every color but think danger is the only end.
"I wish I were a little beast," I'll say, when we go extinct.
Eden crawls around my feet. When we are gone
sky will still refract beyond in the overtaking,
and maybe there will be some waterfalls in it.

IF ALL THINGS WERE THE SAME

It wouldn't be a shame
if things were all the same;
relentless comedies instead
of pain, fellowships of lead
so sanguine, and every being
unlike us crazy with feeling.
Wouldn't it be a shame
if all things were the same.

THE RUSSIAN LANGUAGE

Russian letters entangle me in consonants;
B is v and s rides C-curves
floating backwards in the sun.
My son is studying the mechanics of being
independent of me. I am learning Russian
in tandem, derhythming iambs on my tongue.

I was wrong about the colors of the sounds.
Imperfect recitations! Yet merry-go-rounding
children making finite sentences of infinite words
acoustic and linguistic, linguistic and acoustic.
Daily practice is a watchful going, going—
flung phonemes enchanted with their minds.

I recite my way to heaven, pretending
to be young, but still on page one,
amending speech, and matching sounds
to memories when love was rose-orange
sundowns and noise was grand.
Language came so easily once.

Everything, everything! любовь, love.
I memorize half the letters and shelve the book.

Time for cantos, uplift, singing, letters that are mine.

If I interrupt my years, because he isn't near,

what words will bother to inquire about me

when I am gone, and all my sentences are here?

HAMMERKLAVIER

I

The city blows fireworks into treatises of love
so fine you'd think we were illuminated,
happier in Latin and illustrated at our best angles.
Fire-escape people exited the tenements in ash and smoke.
They are so rich, their souls grow fur on burned fingertips.
A scientist in the Bronx renames constellations after himself.
Bullet trains enter tunnels after her corpse was cleared.
Upstairs, the pianist hammers out the keyboard skips and knotted
insurrectionist fingerwork. We reinvent our fugues—
Listen to the city swinging the cosmic people in B flat, finer
than days the snow piles up and children fantasia down the parkside hills
so fast you'd think their faces would blow off.

II

Bloodwoman on the front page. Crushed by mania—
not only the man who pushed her but engineering
that blueprinted the city with pulsing industrial moods.
My crystal glass refracts grander designs; I drink my rituals.
Sonata 29 rains down from the ceiling in starts.
I think it is not religious but a way to resist
common ecstasy and dispense a few instructions—

don't play it on a harpsichord, don't assume anything
won't happen, and don't forget: fanfare is where you start
to keep it all vivace later, in the mansions and the projects,
all the places you find one kind of gunfire or another in your face,
world without remedies except the sweat of playing it again.

      III

His fingers are heavy on the keyboard after a gentle peace
arrives between drumrolls. I listen to the feeling of climbing
into your fingers from the suitcase of yourself.
The sonata divides my attention and stitches it together
while I work. I know he has read the front page
because tornadoes, trains, and invading troops are his fingers.
I put my boots on and amble up the hill
by the house with the cactus tree strung with lights all year.
Someone is conducting geese pumpjacking south
and baritone frogs by the frazzle-heather.
Dead leaves weep below the fanfare of branches.
I walk in treeshadows and polyskygons, hands in my pockets.

CROSSING THE TIBER

Each bridge, one after another crossing the Tiber,
fills a rational space above the hourglass path
underneath, and repeats itself all the way to Rome;
that way a road defines itself in asphalt
or breaks into pebbles as you go.

I wheel my bicycle between the marshy edge
and dried-out grasses. A delicate blue heron folds its neck
down, into the revelation it seeks, and, fortified,
it pauses, bows its knees in faith of leap, wing-beat, lift—
and glides into the sky, taking its annunciations elsewhere.

Looking down, I consider the two propellers below my feet
twirling desire forward. Startled, I pause; it unseats me,
the science of spoked wheels, carnage of battlefields,
purple-red Tiber of executions and aquatic wealth.
Do I follow the charms of the next town and the next?

The way back is longer than expected. Outside the fort walls
descending to the river, I am mired in medieval feeling.
Should I cycle on, along the path that seems so pastoral?
My muscles burn. I cannot swim across, and sizzle out,
and lack the strength for the next and next. What is dazzling?

I turn and pedal my apotheosis feelings up the hill.

HEDGE MAN

The gardener climbs a ladder, wiring floodlights
in to snip the darkness off and save us.
We think we are so rich, below hedges
trimmed; we believe in Galileo because we telescope
objects of desire and confirm their centrality.

We have lived here since the fourteenth century
We are kings of pencil shavings and paper
gaming high designs; we word-build
in Scrabble and weep over apocalypse letters
that won't weave mechaniv into E or zock in O.

The floodlights swallow all the stars
we loved so much, but made within its shimmer
spotlights of our faces, dissolving behind us
with words and shapes we made at our tables,
knowledge in hand, believing we are so rich.

RHODODENDRON & THE MAPLE

All afternoon, pink petals flung about,
saddling seasons of new fruit to scent
the mellow air all the way to heaven.
Tackle-shadow crowds the patio. Ivy spills
over the fence; long days to think, and love,
and mourn the maple that shaded the garden stones.

It only takes a turn of mind to imagine
a tree inside its absence, so quantifiable
with lemon leaves and bark that smelled
like prayer warming after hibernating months.
The tree threw branches to my son
who made crowns from leafy twigs.

"I am the king of here!" he sang.
I watched him in a dream.
So long since rhododendron and maple
rustled together and the patio smelled
of humid afternoons crawled over
with the sticky mess of beetles and worms.

They gossiped in the sun and shared their soil.
She sashayed pink tresses and dresses all spring.
They talked of pedicel fuzz and divets in the bark,

new life crowning up the filament to the anther,

nearly sprung; the cambium producing cells

for newer xylem, and resin bitter to the tongue.

It was a little bit of an apocalypse;

chain saw buzzing, hatchets thwacking.

Tree limbs trapezed in air.

Sawdust gusted everywhere.

The rhododendron is bigger than ever.

Women are wearing dresses again.

SURVEILLANCE CULTURE

In the hereafter, years divide in table-of-contents style.
We read with monitor eyes, we breathe electrified.
Philosophies of lost-and-found people are anarchy at best
lies to write on tombstones explaining (to whom?) our lives.
We trudge to beaches for sunshine, bury our feet in coffins of sand.
This is what exists outside of hospitals and the dying:
Gold, fever, patience, charity, society, minerals, vapor, love
high above the tree line.

                  Tell me what I will miss most.
To be an unusual person, to be kind; is it better
to bloody the pavement with fleshy disappointments
or balm my tiny sidewalk with love so pronounced
it melts the identical identities that ratio our tired minds?
We were never inherently fractional people.
I want to believe we are outliers like every fingerprint
made in the womb; I wish to believe there is no watchdog society
inking our behavior in zeros and one or photographs archived
in boxes labeled: wrong beliefs, wrong skin, wrong ideas.

                  I am always wrong if I am always right
in the bitter matchstick of my mind, where nothing glows but fire
which has something to do with love, but is irrational; it rations
my own awareness of sensitive data that piles up;
in the larger scheme I am no better than algorithms that turn
honorable truths inside out, that prioritize what worlds like

most; these are not the trajectories that speed-of-light irregularities
wanted us to know. What is handworked should be a mood—
a ceramics-soul, lithographs of laughter and delight,
drawing that is quantum, writing in sky that diction-verbs forever.
                              Love is a ticket to heaven, we think,
but who can see the universe? When you pinball into mystery—
well maybe Hopkins was right: to be is wingbeat-God breathing
in things obvious: falcons or falconer, it doesn't really matter who
or what we are; what matters is that we muse unfettered
and synthesize wrong notes we half-hear with skeptical hearts
into beats—time-stamped truth or a cue to stomp our feet.

DANSE À GRANDE VITESSE:
ONE DANCER HIDES ANOTHER

One dancer hides another

inside the landscape of the turning body.

She twists, like DNA, down his shoulders, chest, hips.

                    It is nothing you can ever see

clearly: One dancer hides another, one choreographer hides another

after the blur of leaving and the enigma of arriving.

Every lift, kick, lunge, and turn blossoms open

in big skies over ancient towns:

Toulouse, Lyon, Limoges, Rouen, Rennes—

locomotion in their toes and lips, the grand life

where something, in the work of moving, emerges.

There is a finale to it: 52 arms swinging, 90-degree knees.

Some speed forward, others, in a blur, recede.

Pairs of dancers move like energy in the sea;

one fixed, the other free. Station-stops on a stage,

one dancer still hides another, all dancers hide their partners.

The body turns three ways at once in its committed

reticulated logic, muscles streamlining, sky-open, up

if asymmetrical in feeling; this is the love of morning

radiance in the evening, the negotiation of blur and fantasy

in hard-earned studio-worked practice-improved lift

eighteen times an hour over seasons during which clouds
    slowly shift their performance;

            really it is a finale of passionate determination
to be en pointe forever, this woman so precise she is nearly
quantum the way she breaks moments into their parts
and, revealing her command of hesitation,
falls
    into her partner's polygon of arms; he catches her
                                leap of faith
and in their rehearsal of disaster they hide the ways
in which they are still discovering one another.

IF YOU COULD SEE THE WORLD FROM HERE

I lift myself up, battle myself down,
write down symptoms of love to prove
  we are, I am, you feel, I do.

My mood traces my shadow searching for itself—
tacklespirit in motion, wind-scaw and bark exploding
branches, love, leaves
        everything happens at once
says the Old Testament and the physicists.

You have to fill your cartilage ears with harmonies
of chainsaws and the claw of useful verbs.

Melodies are at the gate. Gibberish and gyrations
gamble off their troubles, loosed into a better world.

Remove your skeleton and put it here.
Become snow in the soil of the mesa you discovered last year.

Your reversal is not the end of anything.
Clouds shimmer over the foothills where you wander,
Precambrian shade in shallow hills.

What do you see, arriving here?

Stories inside stories.

Incantations falling up the sky from sea.

A seizure in the mind is a cog in the design.

Our joints are acrobatic but not the soul—

ARRIVING IN LA FORTUNA

An orange butterfly opened its wings
a little wider than expected.
Mornings unfolded on cue:
   hot fog parted at noon,
   light swept in with a yellow broom.
Birds catcalled, safe from my inquisition.

Springwater sprung and spilled over.
Land was heated from within,
upsurges from a vast network of churches
   rivering below the rainforest
   singing hymns, bubbling or boiling—
forever baptism or Phlegethon of horrors—

A fer-de-lance, no thicker than a pencil,
eyed us from a bush outside the bedroom.
The plantation is set in forest, they warned.
   Pineapples heavy in their crowns
   reeked, rotting near a swamp eating its banks.
Ducks ran screaming, flapping about love.

Hieroglyphs hung on a penumbra of sunlight
like people dressed up in lost languages.
Steel bridges saved us from abyss

after abyss; hidden and free
we swung from tree to bloody tree.
Monkeys tried to interpret our sentences.

Seeking experience, we crowded
into the local church, concrete and white,
reciting in Spanish the Roman service.
  All the women wore bright skirts.
  We discovered our future
was underground, splashing and celebrating.

ON SEEING FRA ANGELICO'S ANNUNCIATION

An altarpiece measures what is illuminated
beyond binder and pigment, egg and color, woodgrain, brushstroke.
The first time I saw it, at nineteen, I thought art was a way of becoming
composed of techniques an object will turn into; being
inside what you are seeing is as immediate as truth gets.
This was the story of my body, and all women's bodies, to give
life and liveliness to thoughts. I was startled then,
as now, enchanted this pious friar loved with equal tenderness
paint, glazes, tempera, gold, brushes, natural light,
and believed, in a marriage of materials and geometry,
god's word could be told through science and still be right.
From the perspective of perspective, it's just a story on a grid.
From left to right are paradise, angel, woman, and the dove
riding diagonal gold light that sears the painting in two

    45-degree triangles

                        freeze-frame except this lightning
In the left corner, Adam and Eve, naked and glorious,
hurry out of paradise. Gabriel bows to Mary in the foreground,
wings open; so much a creature, with muscular purple-brown feathers.
Delicate Mary receives him in the loggia, the main act and a kind of test
to be tasked with seeing Mary recoil a little to be told instead of asked,
the way we all recoil a little at her task, and then look closer.
Mary sits amplified and queen-like below indigo arches distributing
the weight of the moment, the architecture of the moment;

Corinthian columns between the arches divide

the expulsion from Gabriel and Gabriel from Mary;

technique is all: Vertical lines steer your gaze straight to heaven

(freedom is predetermined, but you can do what god knows already)

while haloes, arches, roundels between the columns, their curved backs

facing one another bracket between them the dove

entering the soft folds of her cascading robes—

In the act of viewing, you enter the orbit of the composition.

                        A penitent old wood bench

                    foreshortened

                        anticipates some need

as if Mary will faint, but its positioning

hints that religious feeling is equal to the leap of faith

painting took in 1420, when linear perspective found truth

arranging our physical bodies in two-dimensional space;

polygons retreating further back inside the canvas

and yelling in triumph: look how science

reveals the organized world. I keep looking past Mary

at that bench in the entrance where later she will sit alone and shake,

unsure if she is saved from the end of peril or the beginning of love.

The arrival of perspective adds dimension to the design

of humankind. We are closer to the beginning

            in this way also a beginning.

                    Art interprets science

                            science explains art.

I have looked at the painting in my mind for thirty years.

How long since that evening-hour when I, nineteen,

set about making passionate sense of my obsession

with annunciations, and the conclusion I was left with then

and now is how awesome and preposterous it is, the workings of the body,

Gabriel's expectation and Mary's promise, Adam's expectation

and Eve's broken promise, for Eve wanted what we wanted—

to be loved for her mind and not her rib, to have knowledge

and someone to share it with. Fra Angelico puzzles it out—

depth of vision, sleight-of-eye, nimble hand.

He recognized that life is, for all its confusions, primarily spatial.

We, the inconstant ones, he set outside the frame, waiting

for us to discover that truth is the story of our lives,

and it exists on a grid; lines hold our compositions together,

lines train our eyes to zigzag, lines interrupt texture,

and the imagined futures constructed inside the lines

trace the actions of our mothers, their sturdiness of heart.

CIVITELLA LIBRARY, ITALIAN SECTION

In the operatic corner in the library,
Italian dialects heckle one another—
whose language is honey
on the tongue and who has disjointed
heads off syllables on the pikes of the invaders—
"Ma ti, vècio parlar, rezìsti."
("But you, old idiom, resist," Zanzotto says)
Everything *dopo*, not a centralizing now but the truer *after*—

We grow old and brittle as these pages
turning on the shelf,
looking for meaning in languages
bigger than our tongues.

Italians in the corner mutter among themselves
while we scrawl our names in the ledger,
a book of history about what,
over many years, people cared about.
They see us march off with armfuls of books,
elated to create the annual harvest of ourselves,
and shake their heads, so many of them
untranslated; so much there is trellising the lyrical
sense we flutter off with.

Answers you seek hide in pages that love you not.
Spines creak open anyway between my hands.

Mosca of Montale's heart
announces herself at the market.
He has numbered all his conversations to her
in poems saturated with loss so alive
she herself picks the fruit he desires that evening—
prickle pears and fennel go home with him
—just a few nights until the almond cake is ready.
Always this system of enduring and making do with.

Sentences stage a riot. They insist they are primary,
not primitive. Susurrations of the sublime in scribblings
untranslated, seeking transit of the life and not the page.

SOUND CROSSING TOBACCO FIELDS

My mouth is filled with rocks, percussive cracks

—timpani, hammer, gravel—

distortions of the mind at work

inside mechanics of mind orchestrating

what the body gives us, plural and uncaring,

to work with.

Typewriter feet gravel by potted lemon trees at the gate;

I descend into raked, chopped-sea tobacco fields,

a rooster struts the path and startles me.

Sun-chandeliers brighten every turn,

tillage and harvest; a weed spikes up, yelling

"marry me in charred remains"

Long light inclines across the ridge all afternoon; hours

yield Mary's dragons, silver-winged surprises in the process of

making-cycles, syllables, eternity

just past apocalypse, and don't nonsense-it;

the gate is locked for a reason; no operating

order of love or love of order—

always this funeral inside me: will it end

before my song is over? Where are my lyrics?

       My ears ache. I hear bell-clanging only

all these campaniles charge straight up

like chimneys, smoke loosening in air—

       sound travels there—

THE CAGED SKYLARK REFLECTED ON A GREEN VASE

I'd been sitting at the table, feigning diligence, though my mind
was ricocheting between tumults that have become, for all their toil,
procedural. The year was so off-kilter that you'd think
some river god, like Skamander in the Iliad rising up to kill
killer Achilles for damning up his watercourse with corpses,
would flood our world and hide the living. I put the book down,
distracted at my distraction as usual. I stare at the sea-green vase
my son made, always ahead of my gaze at the table,
and consider how the glaze gets heavier near the rim.
It changes the color just enough to remind me color is made
of more than one thing. It could be green tea, seaweed, mint,
fern, the bluest soft green of the Indian ring-necked parakeet.
The rim craters as if ash and fire once poured out, which is
a little like firing the piece in a kiln and waiting for what emerges
as it cools. I stare and turn my head sideways at the light-designs
rolling over the surface, and realize Hopkins' verses
are reflected in the vase like torn-off wings. The Caged Skylark
is unintelligible and the stanzas are blurred and upside down—
                              I have read the poem a hundred times
but now I glance at the vase my son made and the words nest
and *prison* hit me with wild rage, because all year we were
scanted in our house cages and time cages while streets
spilled blood and unseasonable shades appeared in Hades.

But one day, my son took to the wheel again, and from clay
extruded this vase. Well, I hadn't put all the pieces together,
but what is art if not an object you labor over and cast in fire?
A kiln is hotter than a cremation chamber. How quick
our bodies turn to ash and then to earth; how strange
we fashion clay from our bones from ash in earth.
I wonder if it's all too macabre to talk about, and decide
it's important that art takes place at a higher temperature
than burning the dead. I gaze down from the glaze,
at the poem on the page. The caged skylark retreats
into the book I snap shut. How beautiful is the house I built
with feathers, sticks, and love. My son turned seventeen last month.
The vase will stay perched here on the table when he leaves,
but he will have all my sentences reflected on him.

TRIOLET ON THE JAMES WEBB SPACE TELESCOPE

It folds ten billion dollars into origami.
Sun-shields blossom and mirrors unfold a dream
to burn a course beyond low-earth orbit, to orbit Sun
it folds ten billion dollars into origami;
a telescope to scout prehistory and void a million miles out
to see, beyond light, formations of the earliest galaxies
it folds ten billion dollars into origami.
Sun-shields blossom and mirrors unfold a dream.

TWENTY-YEAR ANNIVERSARY

Watch my propellor arms
roll my bones over gray waves,
this gentle ebbing a reminder
nothing is ever steady long.

Warm pocket, cold pocket.
    How buoyant our bodies
      jittering across daybreak
        on our twenty-year day.

Shade, you roam in shade,
arms full of landscape
telling me landscape isn't this exactly.
Life is slipperier than I think.

Light ticks west across the lake.
We are sand-drift and leaf-smell
all day together. You swim and say
it is not all sunk to be eternity.

"I want to be a lake."
"But I told you to be blue."
Twenty years have gone.
It isn't up to you.

FIVE SHOTS

I

It is Sunday and a hunter fires five times
—each beat ricochets between shots—
followed by the quieting beat of life
draining in a spray of blood and buckshot.

Dogs circle below the discombobulated pheasant
scissoring down past the cemetery, across the slow road
of engine-rattle and bicyclists burning up the hill
enraptured with the middle way of where they're going—
purposes of travel or reconciliation of the mind.
Wives hanging laundry in the yard
glance up and return to their clothespins and ropes.

The pheasant bobs and jerks as if tracing stairs
in the sky, where heaven is surely waiting
to puppeteer an apotheosis or transfiguration.

II

A child pauses in a field, unsure if his foot
hitting the soccer ball was his firepower or his neighbor's.
He thinks he sees something falling.

Distracted, he wanders to the terrace urn
to see if snails have showed up since it rained last night
and whether slugs are out again.

Their stark sticky thicknesses of being are so straight
it seems like nothing would deter them from their occupation
of waiting in the dirt to be eaten by a beetle
or chomping on his mother's lettuce in the garden,
grown to be consumed.
Unlike the snail, its shell is internal.

He investigates the wild tentacles
cartooning out from a slug's head, and searches for sticks
to stick in his hair in resemblance to the mollusk that seems
not to fear him even as he murders it.

The pheasant banks left over an olive grove and the fence
secluding us here, and the hunters sigh in irritation
because air is free but land does not belong to everybody.

It settles on a grassy slope and remembers
disappearances in season when men with orange plumage
flicker like giant fireflies, and, thinking it is night,
it dies immediately. Someone calls a gardener
who examines it with interest and brings it to the cook
who defeathers it for dinner, humming with pleasure
over the serendipity of a bird in the middle of a journey

across the valley she drove this morning
after bringing her children to school for their lessons.

By now the slug is dead and the snails have retracted
into their nautilus shells. Dogs sniff out a new occasion,
boom, a partridge drops, and barks and cheers ring out.

THINK IS THE PERCUSSION

All day foraging. I wrangle with my text,
art being how it wants, and feel
think is the percussion of thought.

It felt so easy to feel, knives-up grass,
bonfires up north, me banging out varieties
of beings unhinging themselves.

What is dearest always ends up being
true—; more than you reading this white page
or ideas you screw it into.

Watch our asymptote dialogue curve away
and don't bother arguing yourself out of hell
or into heaven. Each has an idea for you.

CANON NOT A LEICA

To talk about old love is to desire up
percussion to another beat, lampooning
struts and striding with giant knees
chattering. To your Leica imagination
here is a silver-sequined dancer muscling
her whoosh on ice, clutching ankles in a twist
before the slurry shoulders she swoons with.
If you looked away, you'd miss it.

Film crosses the street with lightpockets
unannunciated and annunciated, tracked low
to the ground, to the sky, to silver trains
racketing their way across the letter lines,
the way a manual wind-up hand touches
a mind scrolling through its double
debates and triple exposures, knocking
at the door | do you know me from before?

We run the natural world off the landscape
to a page that magically objectifies.
What is futurology if not shutterboxing
inverted life? Briefly it or we are beautiful
stills, caught in a swoon on ice with a certain
complex Leica light. Freeze-framing

is forever, to *hold*, for when it's all over
memories are slurry inside the color photo.

I'll buy a Canon, not a Leica, for paradise
shapes itself from trudging through the muck—
bad lighting, luck, not snapping the *ism*.
Years gave you a jinx of everywhere and ago—
shutterbutton, release, think, snap, know—
but do you see the viewfinder laughing at the show
scrollpapering with people you eyed, and shot,
to keep them whole, and then the scene was lost.

ACKNOWLEDGEMENTS

Many thanks to the editors who have cared about and published these poems, at *The New Yorker, The Kenyon Review, Missouri Review, The Harvard Review, The Kenyon Review, The Notre Dame Review, American Poetry Review, A Public Space, Harvard Divinity Bulletin, Guesthouse Review, The New York City Ballet, The Common, Prairie Schooner, Air/Light, Action Spectacle*, and *Laurel Review*.

I'm elated that Askold Melnyczuk came back into my life with his enthusiasms and wit, and am grateful to be part of the Arrowsmith family. I'm struck by the contemplation and generosity that Ezra Fox put into every detail of the design, editing, and concept, and feel lucky for the many ways he has finely tuned this book. I'm revved to have Catherine Parnell in my life with her fierce and wonderful mind. She is an invaluable conversationalist.

Endless gratitude to friends and family: Jerry Sticker, Ivan Russell, Nina Mehta, James Marcus, Minna Proctor, Dilip Mehta, Edwin Frank, Jordan Smith, Adrian Frazier, Cliff Thompson, Thomas Sayers Ellis, Mary Carlson, Frances Marie-Uitti, Kevin Prufer, and Diane Seuss. Love and thanks to Dana Prescott, Mike and Linda Mewshaw, and Civitella Ranieri for giving me a grand fortune in time that inspired so many poems connected to the Umbrian landscape and the secrets of the castle. At Yaddo I fell in love with the forest full of poisonous mushrooms and glittering puddles and the ferociously intelligent company of other artists. The chance to pay close attention to another artist's work is a gift. Being around other artists in their grooves or grappling with decisions changed my approach.

Diane Mehta was born in Frankfurt, grew up in Bombay and New Jersey, studied in Boston, and now makes her home in New York City. She is the author of the poetry collection, *Forest with Castanets* (Four Way, 2019), as well as a poetics and style guide, *How to Write Poetry* (Barnes & Noble Books, 2005), and the essay collection *Happier Far* (University of Georgia Press 2024-25). Her work has been recognized by the Peter Heinegg Literary Award, the Café Royal Cultural Foundation, a Kirby-Mewshaw fellowship at Civitella Ranieri, and a fellowship at Yaddo. She was the founding managing editor of *A Public Space*, launched and edited Glossolalia for PEN America to publish writing from traditionally underrepresented languages, and was executive nonfiction editor for Guernica.

Books by
ARROWSMITH►
PRESS

Girls by Oksana Zabuzhko

Bula Matari/Smasher of Rocks by Tom Sleigh

This Carrying Life by Maureen McLane

Cries of Animals Dying by Lawrence Ferlinghetti

Animals in Wartime by Matiop Wal

Divided Mind by George Scialabba

The Jinn by Amira El-Zein

Bergstein
edited by Askold Melnyczuk

Arrow Breaking Apart by Jason Shinder

Beyond Alchemy by Daniel Berrigan

Conscience, Consequence: Reflections on Father Daniel Berrigan
edited by Askold Melnyczuk

Ric's Progress by Donald Hall

Return To The Sea by Etnairis Rivera

The Kingdom of His Will by Catherine Parnell

Eight Notes from the Blue Angel by Marjana Savka

Fifty-Two by Melissa Green

Music In—And On—The Air by Lloyd Schwartz

Magpiety by Melissa Green

Reality Hunger by William Pierce

Soundings: On The Poetry of Melissa Green
edited by Sumita Chakraborty

The Corny Toys by Thomas Sayers Ellis

Black Ops by Martin Edmunds

Museum of Silence by Romeo Oriogun

City of Water by Mitch Manning

Passeggiate by Judith Baumel

Persephone Blues by Oksana Lutsyshyna

The Uncollected Delmore Schwartz
edited by Ben Mazer

The Light Outside by George Kovach

The Blood of San Gennaro by Scott Harney
edited by Megan Marshall

No Sign by Peter Balakian

Firebird by Kythe Heller

The Selected Poems of Oksana Zabuzhko
edited by Askold Melnyczuk

The Age of Waiting by Douglas J. Penick

Manimal Woe by Fanny Howe

Crank Shaped Notes by Thomas Sayers Ellis

cont...

The Land of Mild Light by Rafael Cadenas
edited by Nidia Hernández

The Silence of Your Name: The Afterlife of a Suicide by Alexandra Marshall

Flame in a Stable by Martin Edmunds

Mrs. Schmetterling by Robin Davidson

This Costly Season by John Okrent

Thorny by Judith Baumel

The Invisible Borders of Time: Five Female Latin American Poets
edited by Nidia Hernández

Some of You Will Know by David Rivard

The Forbidden Door: The Selected Poetry of Lasse Söderberg
tr. by Lars Gustaf Andersson & Carolyn Forché

Unrevolutionary Times by Houman Harouni

Between Fury & Peace: The Many Arts of Derek Walcott
edited by Askold Melnyczuk

The Burning World by Sherod Santos

Today is a Different War: Poetry of Lyudmyla Khersonska
tr. by Olga Livshin, Andrew Janco, Maya Chhabra, & Lev Fridman

Salvage by Richard Kearney

In the Hour of War: Poetry From Ukraine
edited by Carolyn Forché and Ilya Kaminsky

A Crash Course in Molotov Cocktails: Poetry of Halyna Kruk
tr. by Amelia Glaser and Yuliya Ilchuk

Don't Close Your Eyes by Hanna Melnyczuk

ARROWSMITH is named after the late William Arrowsmith, a renowned classics scholar, literary and film critic. General editor of thirty-three volumes of *The Greek Tragedy in New Translations*, he was also a brilliant translator of Eugenio Montale, Cesare Pavese, and others. Arrowsmith, who taught for years in Boston University's University Professors Program, championed not only the classics and the finest in contemporary literature, he was also passionate about the importance of recognizing the translator's role in bringing the original work to life in a new language.

Like the arrowsmith who turns his arrows straight and true,
a wise person makes his character straight and true.

— Buddha

Milton Keynes UK
Ingram Content Group UK Ltd.
UKHW010721180124
436254UK00005B/515

9 798987 924112